Basics for Relationships

S. J. Meadows

authorHOUSE®

AuthorHouse™
1663 Liberty Drive, Suite 200
Bloomington, IN 47403
www.authorhouse.com
Phone: 1-800-839-8640

First published by AuthorHouse 8/19/2008

ISBN: 978-1-4343-9980-9 (sc)

*Printed in the United States of America
Bloomington, Indiana*

This book is printed on acid-free paper.

Contents

Appreciate Your Significant Other 1

A Love Relationship/not A Competition 2

Arguments In The Bedroom 3

Attractiveness Is Shallow...4

Avoid Desperation...5

Best Friends...7

Check Red Hots...8

Checking Bo Out..10

Communicate Emotions Often 12

Cooking, Cleaning, Doing Laundry..........................13

Discussing Important Issues 14

Do Not Select A Negative Parent..............................15

Do Not Stalk...16

Do Not Use Sex As A Weapon 17

Don't Allow Un-excused Absences.............................19

Dress Not Undress 20

Expectations..21

Fragrances 23

Give Of Yourself/be Supportive 24

I Love You...25

In Love And Venerable 26

It's Okay To Let Go...27

Keep It Real 28

Keeping Focused/not Forgetting................................29

Love Yourself...30

Pone / Those Private Moments 31

Pushing The Envelope 32

Quality Time With Bo 33

Romance Your Significant Other.................................35

Secrets Are For The Two Of You.................................36

Set Ground Rules 37

Testing And Tempting................................40

Travel Solo 42

Vacations/long Weekends Away..................................43

Appreciate Your Significant Other

When your significant other is good to you, say 'Thank you .' When your lover/mate compliments you in any way, say" Thank you." Do not ever take their kindness as a joke. Do not take their kindness for granted. If so, one unexpected day you may regret it.

I was involved in a relationship a few years ago. My significant other never discussed anything with me, concerning us. It was as though our relationship didn't exist. Yet, whenever I distanced myself. They would come around and act out their feels. How sad! One afternoon I just ceased being there.

The cards, letters, candy, flowers, kind words, and other good things ceased. For months my ex mate tried getting back with me. I didn't allow a reunion. For in seeing their negative behavior. I didn't need the drama.

A Love Relationship/ not A Competition

A love relationship is a very valuable phenomenon. So is the person you are in love with. For out of millions you were and are attracted to them. Therefore, you should understand that they mean something to you/the relationship.

So, why is it we compete with one another.?" Why are we at odds many times with our lovers?" Truth is, we have a low self esteem. Hence, rather than be ourselves. We try and become our lovers. We act like them. We sometimes act as though they are our enemies. We in time began overtime to complain of none sense things.

Please understand, you are lovers. This isn't a ball game. It is our happiness. Our way of becoming complete with some one outside ourselves. The complaining, the competing will keep the setting unsteady.

So, what happens when foundations are unsteady? Nothing steady can remain stable. Therefore, others are secretly brought into the relationship. It is then rocky and soon the couple's relationship is dissolved..

Compliments are threads that mend broken hearts. Romance is the glue for holding the relationship together. Then as we learn to lean on one another. Our relationship becomes stable.

Arguments In The Bedroom

You should never argue in your bedroom. It is where you rest, do lovemaking, quality discussions concerning you and yours, nurture your significant other. So, get rid of any unpleasant attitude at the threshold of your bedroom.

Besides, the atmosphere once there is an argument, is filled with negative energy. Energy that will come at you, and cause restless sleep. Then place you in a position of negative thinking. Arguments are triggers that cause us mostly a type of pain. No doubt, because of our own insecurities, we argue. They lock our intellect for a time, as they allow only repetitive negative words to flow. Arguments then make us either survivors or dream killers.

I've been in love a few times. I do not like to argue. I always try to see the other persons point of view. Of course, I'm not perfect, and sometimes have to apologize and ask forgiveness.

Attractiveness Is Shallow

We are many times mislead by what is beauty, and that which is beautiful/attractive. One is beautiful if they have personality, a clean appearance, and have their feet on the ground. Beauty is that which is made with facial makeup, false body parts, and weave/wigs. It is very superficial, and thus, doesn't allow your significant other to get to know you.

I've dated attractive people. They are often shallow, selfish, prideful and extremely materialistic. However, those that capture my attention are the pretty people. You are pretty when your speech, facial appearance, hair, inner strengths compliment your presence.

These people are very rear. They are genuine. They have your back. They live for today. They are usually street smart and extremely educated. A day in the park with you is appreciated. They are beautiful people. They are those who value you for you. If you shall ever meet one, value them.

Avoid Desperation

Desperation whatever form it takes is costly. Consequently, those who are desperate, must be ready to pay a cost for their desperation. You will regret it. Yet it is how it is.

When you are desperate in a relationship. Each thing said is taken at face value. The person compromising will continue to compromise. Please understand, whatever you compromise to keep you will lose. So, do not allow too many mishaps before taking cover. When you hear that a storm is coming. Do you wait to feel the rain drops on your head, before taking cover? I think not.

Therefore, when he/she says he is not pleased with you. Do not think it is hopeless. You should get it totally together. You should focus on you. Then enhance your attitude, and appearance. Ironically most do the opposite. You go into a depression. Then let go of your self esteem, and appearance. Why? Merely because you are in love with him/her. He/she said something to defeat you.

In spite of this, love your self. Do not allow your morals/values to be compromised. No one on earth is worth your dignity. There are a host of Bo's out there. However, if you bury yourself in defeat, you will never see them.

One of the Bo's out there might be the one who will

support you. Who will stand by you when the storm is ragging. Who will have your back no matter the situation. So, again quit being so desperate for a lover/significant other, that you'll do anything. Once you do all respect is gone. They will then dog you out worse than ever. Besides, if someone loves you. They are not going to disrespect you. They will of course, compliment you.

Once when I was in love with someone and I began to write. My significant other wasn't pleased. Bo wasn't supportive. I compromised to keep them. I lose the relationship and didn't write again for ten years plus years. I was desperate to have Bo's love. My cost in time I can't recover. Yet ,I take pleasure in that which I learned.

Best Friends

If at all possible become your significant others best friend. For in doing so you are more tolerant. So, take the time to get to know your lover. Good friends are very difficult to find.

Your responsibility as a best friend, as well as theirs is, to give every pleasure you can. For best friends have unconditional love. They are patient. They are very able to be that sounding board you need from time to time. Best friends continue in the race of life, until the end.

I met a lady serval years ago. She and I became best friends. We are still best friends today. Although, we do not communicate daily/some times yearly. When we talk we are at the point we need to discuss things.

I've lived in five states, the past twelve years. Her phone number has remained the same. I can phone anytime. I can tell her anything that is on my mind. So, this best friend doesn't always have to be a lover/significant other. More importantly, they are for a life time. So finding a best friend is a valuable experience, and is lasting.

I value this friend. I value all best friends. I am blessed to have a few. We talk and discuss situations important to us.

Check Red Hots

The past few months I've heard and read of domestic violence more than ever. It has included ministers, movie stars, and regular families. I believe though ,had they paid strict attention, to the red hots. Most of these situations would have been different.

When you were at your Bo's family reunion, and he/she became angry, because that guy/lady touch your hand. Sweetheart that was a red hot. The next day when the eggs were prepared with cheese, and not with bacon bites. Bo threw the frying pan against the wall. Another red hot, and so on.

Yet, you thought it was funny. For it merely showed Bo cared. Okay! Then that Christmas night around the fire place. When Bo got drunk and fondled the neighbor. You got upset, and he slapped you, once in the bedroom.

Are these scenarios familiar? How they start doesn't matter. What you allow afterwards does. Never allow anyone to abuse you. A slap today unpunished, tomorrow maybe a broken arm or death.

Please do not go into denial. "It was my fault. He had a very stressful day." Whatever he or she had. Doesn't give them the right to abuse you.

Once my temper wasn't very controlled. I learned overtime to modify it. I would get very angry, then later apologize. My significant other would just sit and look. Then say," Okay! you are just going to apologize later." I felt very silly and that particular day promised myself .I'd change my attitude.

The next few months were filled with my learning to control my temper. I had a few battle with myself but, got through.

Checking Bo Out

For a number of years, men have controlled interviews, background checks on women. They have thus dominated the market of background searches. So, why not learn a thing or two ladies.

Mr. Perfect/Ms. Perfect should be investigated. He/she is in your life. They are in your life/your house. What do you know about Bo?

You can spend a few dollars and do a background check. You can hire an investigator, to check Bo out. Yet, I say date him/her. If you do not allow them to come to your house ,half the battle is already yours. At least, then if you aren't please. He/she doesn't have permission to visit you.

Another thing while checking Bo out, only give the cell number to him/her. They are an interest that you have. They can live without knowing every detail. You should also not deny important information given you. Such as jail time they may have done. Of course, find out details by asking him/her.

I keep using him/her yet, in having lived in five states. I have found due to being in management ,and performing background checks that. Often the ladies in certain geographic locations, have more felonies / misdemeanors that guys.

So, lets not get twisted as we assume who's at fault most. The young ladies seem to fight more over the guys. The guys according to many years of counseling, get tired and just start another love relationship. In essence, the guys do not worry concerning who, what when where and how.

The guys did in some western states seem more dependent on their ladies than in others. Someone once said,"We love our son's and raise our daughters." Perhaps! One thing is certain, if we date Bo for a time, all important issues will present. How we deal with our relationship issues, is determined by our general life long orientation.

Lastly, you can find out where Bo is employed ,and visit him/her there. For certain their employment is real. This is also a testimony, as to how stable he/she is. For instance, if he/she has more than one year employment. They are usually stable with employment.

Communicate Emotions Often

I recently met a very beautiful person. One who communicates extremely well. What a blessing. For many years I've had to pump information from my mates/ significant others. They were either too busy, too afraid of what they might hear, or just not good communicators.

If you need help communicating emotions, get before a mirror. Say what you need to say, and get good at it. Then talk to your mate/significant other. I bet you will feel better. However, do give them a chance to talk as well.

Polish your social skills. Rehearse your conversation, articulate well. Do not tell others to talk for you. Many times that person will become the other person in the relationship. Their talking eventually will lead them to favor the person you are discussing. So, people be aware.

E-mail is fine, telephones too, but, do not make them a way of constant communication. These devices build false images. The actual conversation one on one gives clues and show ones true expressions.

I have someone I'm very interested in. They communicate very well, and is attentive. I show my appreciation as often as I can. I believe we will have a lasting relationship.

Cooking, Cleaning, Doing Laundry

These chores are universal. Yet , most guys, boyfriends ,husbands, Feel they are in secular duties meant for a woman. How absolutely sad. I believe that the duties should fall to the person getting home first. Then to the other person who arrives home later. You should ASAP assist with everything.

Society has said, "That A woman's place is in the kitchen, bedroom, and in the church." That well maybe but, women are in congress, the senate, the white house, the courthouse, and so on.

So guys who are not sure of your duties. It is okay to help around the house. It is okay to wear an apron." For I believe that real men wear aprons anyway."Remember when Mom was sick, and dad worn the apron an he cooked breakfast, lunch and dinner. So, figuratively then real men also wear dresses as well.

Macho men do not panic. It is okay to cry as you, help out around the house. For your masculinity isn't measured by your household duties. It is only measured by the content of your character.

Discussing Important Issues

When possible make certain you select a person, who is equal to you. If they are intelligent, you should be as well. For when issues present, you will have a built -in support system and advisor. So, choose very well. Your issues are things that are inevitable. You should not have to discuss them with outsiders. Your business is private, keep it as such. Please make certain to look your partner in the eye, when talking. Listen attentively, and interject with extreme care, and concern.

Do Not Select A Negative Parent

When selecting a significant other, do not select someone like your negative parent. Nine chances out of ten, we will due to orientation, select someone exactly like that parent.

This is true due to as I have said the familiar. That which we saw growing up, is what is etched in our intellect. However, the reconditioning of our minds when we are born again, many times can alter this behavior. Otherwise the alcoholic dad/mom, is vividly seen in the selected husband/wife. The exact nagging, and profanity, are other confirmations. Not to mention the physical abuse, and infidelity.

Do Not Stalk

Stalking no matter what form it take, is illegal as well as insane. Besides, shows an extreme amount of insecurity. Your self esteem is close to zero as well. Why? Maybe due to your cheating. Perhaps due to your inability to satisfy your significant other.

Whatever your reasons, get it together. You are causing your mate/partner discomfort. Not to mention, yourself appearing insane to your peers and friends.

I had a stalker for two years. Who used facial masking, wigs, and other form of disguises. My first thought was maybe it is Halloween again. Perhaps, they are having a masquerade party somewhere.

Then as time passed I mentioned this behavior to my significant other. A pause was quickly made. The ex changed to another disguise, and on and on. This behavior continued until I ended the relationship.

I believe the ex is seeking help for a previous traumatic situation. I wish them well, as I pray for their recovery, don't stalk.

Do Not Use Sex As A Weapon

Sex/lovemaking are not to be used as a weapon. If you withhold sex/lovemaking to get even you are not correct. Stop the drama! For if you think it is okay, just listen in the beauty shops/barber shops. The gossip there is mind-boggling and very detailed.

Often times someone in the midst is sleeping with someone you know. It is the law of the jungle, to have an affair for some. For a very few others it isn't taboo to cheat.

Once when I was very naive. I thought love last forever with most. Reality appeared and I became a victim of heartbreak. The sting of infidelity was a moment I will remember. Yet ,I will keep falling in love. I believe it is a way of ultimate survival. It is a way of becoming, more in reality than we are when alone.

Besides, if you use sex/lovemaking as a weapon. The needed person across town/next door, is more than willing to service your mate/significant other. This is a warning for church folk, as well as secular people. Please do not deceive yourself, into thinking you are preventing sexual pleasure. If you use sex as a weapon. For if one is determined to dance. They will dance with those available.

Again I believe in monogamy. Consequently, my

mate/significant other do not have to worry. If I have to catch an extra plan home from lectures/booksignings. I will do it to stay loyal. My relationship is very valuable . I appreciate my friend.

Don't Allow Un-excused Absences

If your significant other is forever tardy, find out why. Do not except a non response. This is often an avoidance to keep secrets. If you can't get an answer, leave the mess. You will find peace, outside your relationship.

This may appear hard. Yet, if you stay you will see countless flaws as time presents. Your mate is not honest, and the silence is to appease their guilty.

Once upon a nightmare, I married A Silent Player. This character was so good at home. I never had to put my shoes on. I never had to prepare most meals. I was allowed to come home for one year and not work. Wow!

I was rudely awaken when the other woman visited our home. I loss control, and between the police coming and whatever else. The other woman was rescued.. Two days later my ex had moved in with the next victim.

Two months later my ex wanted to return . I moved to another state to rid myself of the ex. So pay strict attention to the signals of infidelity: un-excused absences, needless arguments, your mate begins to dress differently, a new hairdo, use of a new fragrance, and so on.

Dress Not Undress

When someone is looking for a significant other. They do not wish to find a bad girl./guy. They wish to find someone who will compliment their personality. Someone who will support them, and make a positive difference in their life. Therefore, dress in a fashion that will compliment yourself/your mate.

Low cut revealing clothes, be they men or women isn't always appropriate for all. Some fashions are for the young only. Others should be worn very well, when worn They should compliment your body. Clothes should not reveal scared body parts. For if everyone can see your body it isn't precious to you nor your significant other.

Another disrespect are some tattoos, especially the Tramp Stamp. You know the tattoo that can be easily seen from the low rider pants. The one that covers the lower back just above the buttocks. Tattoos are fine. However, when they encompass precious body parts, such as I have stated. They are to be viewed by your lover/significant other only. So lets keep it real. You should wear what compliments you/your significant other. If your mate/significant other is pleased, that is the ultimate, blessing to you.

Expectations

I'm delighted to write this book. It is one I seriously feel is long over due. I believe our expectations govern our outcomes in our relationships. Consequently, what we think and tend to expect we act in such a fashion, we cause it to become our reality.

Some call this a self fore filling prophesy. I call it scared of history repeating itself. Once we allow emotions from our past to crowd our future relationships. We abort the relationship. Although we stay and pretend all is very well. Our love relationship is seriously over.

Resurrection of the same is impossible. Once an old friend had married a young lady, ten years his junior .She after his nagging began an affair with her boss. My friend found out about the affair. He and his young wife divorced.

He after several months, remarried this young lady. They fought almost nightly. He stated to me one day,"San, I will not allow her to forget she cheated on me." My reply was,"Very few people willingly walk back into an accident, after the first wreck. You sound as though you purposely, remarried this lady. Why? So that no one else could date or have sex with her? You are not being fair to her."

My old friend after this , married one of his employees.

Of course, ten years his junior again. This lady was the mother of two children. He later stated," San, you were correct. I wanted to punish my ex for hurting me. I'm cool now."

I often wonder if he is happy now. For very often as we have a vindictive personality. We treat every relationship the same. We only change if we realize, it is ourselves who are mainly at fault.

So do not allow the mess from other relationships to handicap you. The getting even attitude is more harmful to you, than others. So expect the best, Okay.

Fragrances

I was told by a fragrance expert more than ten years ago." A fragrance is on correctly when others can smell it and you can't." So, ladies/gentlemen do not over due with the fragrances.

There are times when shopping a person will walk in my space. The odor will almost overwhelm you. So pick your fragrances well, give your significant other, something nice to enjoy.

For various smells can be sensual and sexy. Your body chemistry determines the delivered aroma.

Give Of Yourself/be Supportive

The mere act of giving has to do with the law of reciprocity. It is scriptural as well(Luke 6:38KJV). If we are generous we receive good seed back.. So, give of yourself. This can mean supporting your mate/significant other 's work/career. It can mean encouraging them. It can mean being candid, as you support their dreams.

If your mate/significant other is in a career/job, support them without nagging. The last thing they need to hear, if they are super busy is ,"Honey, you need to spend more time with me." Grow up! If they aren't cheating, they need you to understand. When this isn't the case, you are stressing them to an uncomfortable level. Thus causing their job to be more of a chore.

Encourage them with kind words. Encourage yourself with the same. You would be amazed how often we forget to be kind to those we love. It is shameful. It is one thing everyone need.

Lastly, support their dreams. Charity/love suffereth long, and is kind , envieth not; vaunteth not itself,is not puffed up,(1Corinthians 1:13-4).

I Love You

I love you. A phase voiced since the world was formed. It is often applied to a person, place or thing. There are several kinds of love: erotic love, physical love, and parental love/agape.

I believe erotic love hedge on sexual passion, is not meant to last very long. When this is the case, the person involved are usually promiscuous. For the more sex gotten, the more is needed.

Physical love is when I believe you mate with your husbands/wives. It consummates the relationship. This love isn't suppose to be taken lightly.

Lastly, agape is a God kind of love."For God so loved the world, that he gave his only begotten Son. that whosoever believeth in him should not perish, but have everlasting life,.(John 3:16 KJV).

Not all relationships are consummated with physical love. For some love relationships are plutonic. All the traits of the love relationship are there. However, sex isn't. I can attest to this type of relationship.

More than two and a half years ago I fell in love with someone. There wasn't any lovemaking. Yet the pain of the breakup was just as devastating. The recovery time was just as needed. The closure just as necessary.

In Love And Venerable

How many times have I been told that love makes one venerable. It is okay to be venerable . Of course, make certain it is with the person God has chosen for you. If not your life will become a living hell. How can two walk together if they aren't in agreement, (Amos 3:3). If you aren't agreed, there are always those insane little arguments. Those misunderstood words, that should have been understood.

I believe though if we would pray preventive prayers over our situations. We would prevent much of this stuff from happening. The enemy never want to see any relationships work.. The unity in that relationship is so very difficult to disarm. So, he is aware if he divides he can conqueror.

So allow yourself to be venerable. Your love can endure the storms. If you keep the people(gossipers/haters out). So, do not get caught up in peer pressure either. We can become addicted to weakness there, wear your wisdom hat whenever you can.

It's Okay To Let Go

Sometimes when our relationships are over. We find it difficult to let go. Please hear me now. People it is okay to let go. It is definitely okay to move ahead. Those chains that bind us should in due time fall powerless behind us.

When I was in love once. I had difficulty letting go of the person in my relationship. I must have tried three or four times to let go. I would walk back to the relationship, and pick it up again. One day while meditating I got wise. I began to fast and pray. I then asked God to help me move on. For I wasn't capable of letting go, until God intervened.

I do not mean to sound fanatical, just born again. I'm my mother's daughter, and my father's child. I know it is okay now to always move on.

Keep It Real

Authenticity is a very dear value seldom seen in relationships today. The best foot forward method is mostly used. Then when time cause ones patience to fade the relationship goes into a spin.

Save the needless, drama. Tell him/her if you are in love with someone else. If you are bi-sexual, homosexual, heterosexual or A sexual. Honesty is the best policy.

Keeping Focused/not Forgetting

When love has passed you by, and there is no hope for it in your life. You have to stay focused. If not you'll find your self drifting towards folk you do not need in your life. So focus and do not forget, what you learned from that love/plutonic relationship.

Once your relationship has end. Do not forget to do a make over on yourself, change your hair style, buy new and fun clothes. In other words make yourself more attractive. It is one of the ways you can get attention from others. I also believe a nice fragrance is needed as well.

Do not spend too much time dwelling on the old relationship either. Bo is gone on his way. He/she is now with someone else. So , keep yourself looking well. He/she will eventually see you and think." My he/she is looking extremely well. I missed out."

Then although you might be going through a hell that is undescribable. He/she will never know. Your appearance is one thing that can be deceiving, the best to you.

Love Yourself

Love is when we decide to share with a self outside ourselves. This person is usually our opposite. Yet ,we love them. We often forget about ourselves. Love to us then is how we care concerning our lover. What about us though?

Falling in love with yourself is the best thing since chocolate chip cookies, and vanilla ice cream. Yet, most folk do not understand how. We are often taught to love others, and not love ourselves ,because it is selfish.

I disagree. Loving ones self teach us to be good at nurturing. So, does being in a relationship. Often harsh treatment to ones self, signals abuse in other areas. So love instead of pain. For you should always remember, you deserve the best.

Pone / Those Private Moments

Pone in your relationship cause one to falter. He/she is destined to venture out and find a new mate. Besides, spend lots of time in the restroom. So, make certain you and your significant other, and consistent.

First find out what is liked concerning the pone. Then remove it ,but replace it with yourself, and their fantasy. Of course, as long as it doesn't go against your beliefs. Again, do not compromise values, to fill a fantasy. You will lose the relationship anyway.

Phone sex is another fantasy that is costly. Often times performed in the privacy of the home. Again find out why? Then if you can fill the fantasy, do so." God Bless You and Yours."

Pushing The Envelope

Who will manage the money? In actuality the money is controlled by the finance department(whomever is better qualified). All money for the family should be put together, until determined how it will be used. However, always have a savings for yourself and your mate.

One good way to do this is take the major salary for bills. Then the lower salary evenly divide, into each savings. This way everyone is being paid..

Do not buy items and keep them on the shelf. Once I did this a lot with household goods. I had to cease doing so. I had many dollars tied up on the shelves. These dollars could have been used somewhere else.

Quality Time With Bo

Today most couples work outside their home. Therefore, quality time is rear. When it is managed well couples thrive. Their relationship has vast meaning. They are the center of their universe.

This quality time should be set aside often. It should include only your self and your mate. Those busters that try to intrude, should be told the same. Do not even allow biological family to steal quality time either. If it is for yourself and the wife(or self and your lover). This quality time is precious.

You can instill this concept in your children. Then they are aware of how this quality time is used. If it is quality time for your children, make it a date. Dad take the daughter out for the night. Mom take the son out for the night. This also teach your children how they are suppose to be treated by others. For it is nothing more outstanding, than being the example for your children.

No arguing during this time. You are in one another's presence for pleasure. So, not remembering yesterday 's mess, will keep you centered. Soothing words keep us silent and warm. Hash words damage our intellect, and cause us to remember unpleasant situations.

Besides, battles are won on fields, not in homes and living rooms.

If your mate isn't interested show him/her tactfully with interesting conversation, movies, and such. It is worth the wait. Especially, if you are genuinely in love with your significant other.

Romance Your Significant Other

Romance I believe is our own personal way, in which we decide to be thoughtful and sweet to our significant other. It can be as simple as speaking kind words to them, sending flowers, giving a greeting card, or phoning daily and saying,"I love you."

I love being in love. The newness of the relationship keeps me spontaneous. It does me good to tell my significant other beautiful words. The mere thought of them cause me to smile.

Please remain polite and say,"Thank you and please.'

Secrets Are For The Two Of You

I believe secrets are things meant for ourselves and our significant others. Consequently, when we reveal them to others they become gossip. Gossip that isn't complimentary to anyone.

So, bedroom secrets, and others keep them for your quality time. If you must discuss them, they are safe during your mates and your quality time. There the two of you can find a solution,(if one is needed).

Of course, some secrets if they are damaging to your relationship. You should carry to the grave. Especially, those that would cause your lover to view you in a different light. Please do not lie. Those issues of no concern to now, can wait forever. For sometimes we can give too much information, think.

Mama doesn't have to know every detail. She is usually partial to her child not you. So, keep your secrets.

Set Ground Rules

Ground rules are foundational for relationships. If not it is certain one or the other will step out of bounds. Besides, assumptions and uncertainties will keep things off key.

Ground Rules

1.Respect one another	6.No slow dancing
2.Trust your mate	7.No fondling
3.Allegiance to your mate	8.No kissing
4.No flirting with others	9.No name calling
5.No sex with others	10.Good hygiene

Respect merely means, you show favor to your significant other. He/she deserves your best treatment. So, no eyeing others while with your significant other. Everyone will give a look here and there. Looking is innocent. Eyeing is not.

Eyeing for me means, staring without blinking , with a lustful expression. Looking is merely glancing at another person. There is no intent.

Another disrespect is, paying a compliment to others, that is appropriate for your lover/mate. This one can bring unwanted consequences later.

Secondly is trust to me it merely means, confidence

that what is said is the absolute truth. And being able also to leave your significant other anywhere. She/he remains yours, and untouched a month or a year from that time.

Third, giving allegiance to your mate. No matter who is there, they are first.

Forth, no flirting, is supposedly understood.. Yet, people are falling due to the flirting daily.

Fifth, no sex with anyone other than your significant other. I believe in monogamy. One mate at a time. One relationship at a time. For every partner you have, add all of their partners to the picture also.

Six, no dancing slow unless you are with your mate. The closeness, the repetitive touching of bodies against each other, can cause arousal. So, keep it clean.

Seven, no fondling others. This is sexual harassment. It is illegal at the work place, at your house, my house, etc.

Eight, no kissing except with your significant other. Kisses are for mates, They are very needed and needful when showing affection.

Nine, do not call names. This is extremely childish. It causes arguments. Our words are like weapons. They hurt, and carry scares.

Ten, good hygiene an elementary thing. Yet, so overlooked sometimes. I met an alcoholic several years ago. He and I were discussing hygiene. He laughed saying." I use hygiene to keep my wife away. She doesn't like it when I'm drinking. She tells me I stink."

"My how sad." I replied.

"My breath, my dirty body after a few days. Is my defense against her. She is so proper . My wife can't stand me after several days of drinking. I get to stay away from home with my other lady,"he explained as he laughed.

Anyway! Good hygiene in a natural setting is always favorable. This scenario is off the cuff abnormal.

Testing And Tempting

Tempting and testing your mate/significant other, is what I do not understand. A lady came to me one day. She had been married and was then divorce. She had consented to her then husband having an affair; after she had tempted him with her best friend.

I sat glancing with a concerned expression, as she wept and discussed her experience. I listen as a counselor for a crisis center. I assured her that, she had made the ultimate mistake. She ceased crying then asked,"Can you help me get him back?"

I informed her as a counselor. She left the office and returned two weeks later. A complete alcoholic she had been since her divorce.

Another girl came by the following week and stated her case. "My boyfriend keeps tempting me with his friends. He'll have them call and ask me for a date." I smiled and asked," Are the two of you still together?"

She smiled saying ,"Yes!" I asked her to inform her boyfriend that this irritated her."

She agreed, they discussed his behavior. He continued doing the same.

Two months following this they separate. Two things are happening here, either the guy feels insecure and has a very low self esteem. Or he in involved some place else.

This breakup would allow him to leave. Whatever the real deal, people who are tempting and testing are ill. I would never do a foolish thing such as things done here.

First of all I fall in love with my significant other. I respect /trust them to do that which is correct. I give unselfishly, and romance them. I love them like they should be loved. I feel they are worthy of me too.

Consequently, the only testing/tempting I'm doing with are with my romancing them. So be that as it may, I have no need of tempting/testing, with others.

Travel Solo

Travel alone when hanging out with your friend/lover. Especially, when the two of you seldom spend time together. A group of friends make the setting public. Even if you wished to be intimate, it is not possible.

Avoid advice from those in your group, who do not have a mate/lover. Or those who have a rocky relationship. They are going to be envious, and seldom positive with words. They will hate on you as well as your relationship. So, keep it your private relationship.

Anyway ,groups serve as buffers for insecurity. You may have decided to avoid intimacy, this way. Consequently, you welcome the group. If this is you, please seek help. Your insecurities are keeping you in bondage. Your significant other need you, not that gossiping group.

Vacations/long Weekends Away

I believe that vacations are meant to be enjoyable, relaxing, and filled with fun. They are to be spent with those we love. If not I've missed the point of a vacation. So, lets do our vacation in a very warm and stimulating location.

Your lover/significant other and you should decide on the place. How it will be paid for, clothes needed and so on. Do not make the mistake of visiting war torn countries, for adventure. War is real and so are those bombs and missiles. How boring!

When on vacation take this time to reacquaint yourself with Bo. It astounds me how we overlook small things, of importance. "I love you, thanks, and please "are words we need to hear. You are not you from the outside of yourself. The genuine you is the one on the inside. So, pour out those positive words. Please use good etiquettes.

My compliments to my significant other, are genuine. My increasing love a valued reality, one I continue working on. For real love is like any genuine relationship.... we must continuously work on it.

S. J. Meadows